I Can See Peace
Written by Julie D. Penshorn, MBC
Content edited by Rebecca Janke, M.Ed.
Illustrated by Jeanine-Jonee Keith

ISBN 978-0-9988691-3-1

Library of Congress Control Number: 2018955441

For information on other books, free resources, our blog, and a link to the Songs for Peace album including the "I Smile at Myself" song, please visit www.smarttoolsforlife.com.

First Edition, First Printing, Published by Growing Communities for Peace: Smart Tools for Life

Smart Tools for Life is an ongoing project of the nonprofit, Growing Communities for Peace (501 c3).

www.smarttoolsforlife.com

I CAN SEE PEACE

I can see peace, it's all around me.

I can see peace in the birds, in the trees.

I can see peace in a warm, sunny day.

I can see peace in the stars far away.

I can see peace
in the dog and the horse.

I see peace most
when I'm happy
of course.

I can find peace in a soft gentle rain.

8

Peace can be found
again
and
again.

I can find peace
in a smile

or a look

I can find peace

on the page
of a book.

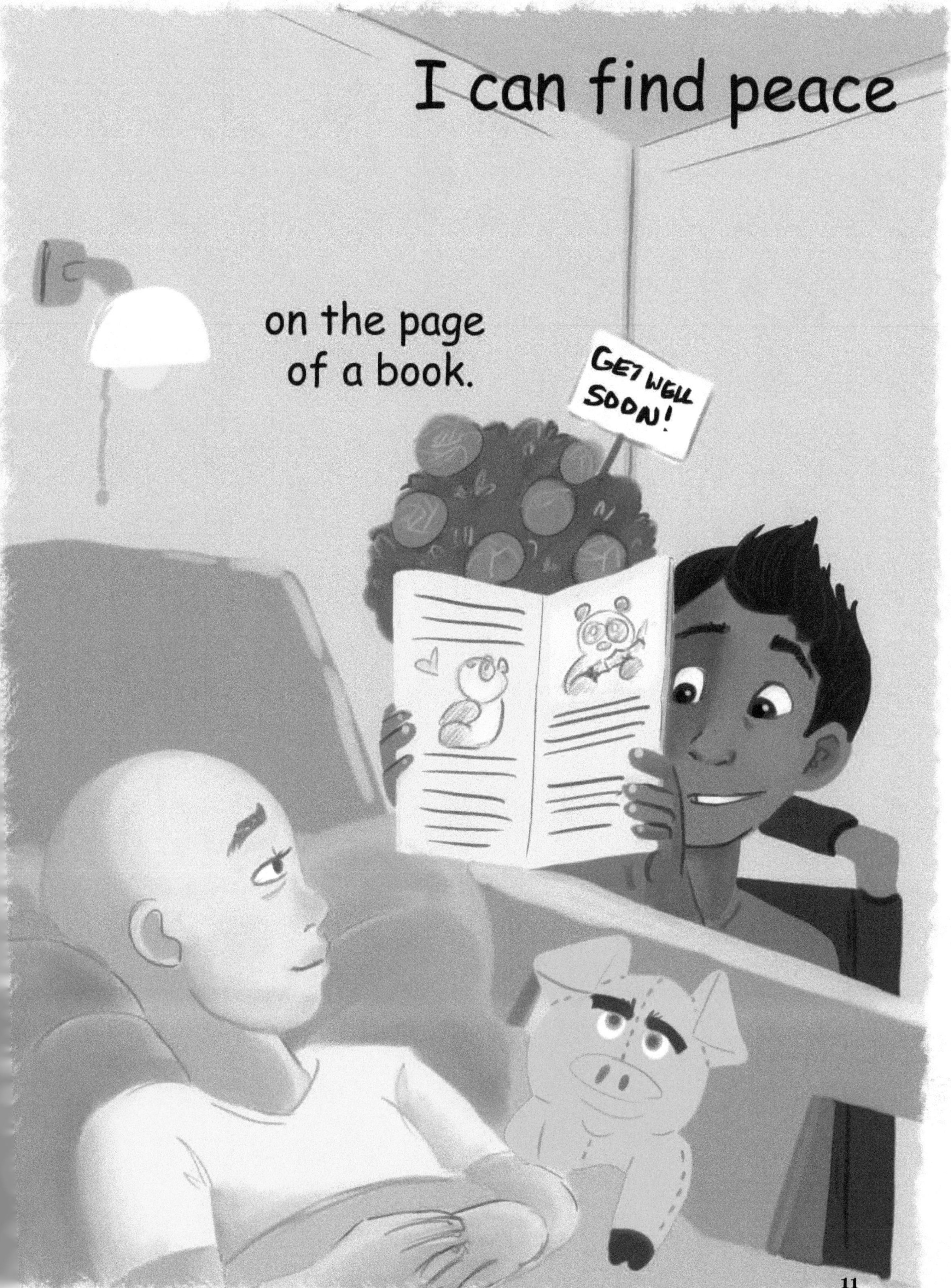

But peace can get interrupted you see...

By nature, by fights. . . in my own family.

But I have the power and wisdom to seek

the tools to solve things peacefully.

I calm myself when I breathe in and out.

Sometimes, I can see peace all about!

I can see peace in my own smile or grin
and then I see peace begins from within.

With love in my heart and peace on my mind,
I can find peace almost anytime.

I may struggle to find peace right now...

21

But if I keep seeking,
I'll find it somehow!

Why this Book

Seeking peace is fundamental to finding it! The journey itself can illuminate the path out of separation and anxiety, toward connectedness, love, and, of course, peace!

The ability to imagine peace and then get back to it when it is interrupted, with tools such as mindful breathing, awareness of the natural beauty of the earth, listening, talking about feelings, and creative problem solving sets the stage for building capable, confident, and happy children who grow up ready to care for themselves, others, and the planet with compassion.

Building a structure around children that we call a culture of peace, is critical! By infusing kids with hope and a sense of belonging at an early age, we believe we support healthy social and emotional skills, enhance mental wellness, and encourage smart choices in life.

Please visit our blog for more ideas and information at www.smarttoolsforlife.com

Enhancing the Learning: Ideas for Guiding Children

The practice of looking for and embracing peace in daily life helps us appreciate it as healthy nourishment for our hearts and minds. Parents, teachers, teen, or adult mentors each bring an interesting and fresh perspective to the reading, and offer a unique way of guiding children to value peace and strive to get back to peace when it has been interrupted.

Seeking, relishing, and treasuring peace contributes to the joy of life. By compiling a foundation of memories, peaceful moments can continue to soothe and comfort, long after the initial experience has passed. Memories like these build resiliency and help children get through difficult times.

Since children are guided by the surrounding culture, including books, music, TV, movies, and games, this book is an important addition to their libraries. The characters in this book show children examples to enhance their learning about peace and make it more concrete.

I Can See Peace has many pages devoted to enhancing children's awareness of the beauty of the planet and its living beings. This theme prompts children to learn to love and nurture the earth and care for its creatures, thus providing a wonderful place to begin a discussion about the effects of our personal choices of food, energy-consumption (simple things like turning off the lights), caring for our pets and other animals, and even recycling. All these, and more, are areas of stewardship where children can participate.

The importance of relationship health is illustrated numerous times in this book as well, thus paving the way for children to value learning about and using peaceful conflict resolution techniques and celebrating each other's diversity. (See *The Barnyard Buddies STOP for Peace* by Julie Penshorn for an age-appropriate conflict resolution process.) With your guidance, they can enjoy an enhanced quality of life as their relationships with themselves, others, and the earth, flourish.

How Do *You* Seek Peace?

Some of the illustrations in this book may remind you of a time you experienced peace. Perhaps for you, peace is the soft touch of a baby's cheek or a grandma's welcoming smile. Does your heart fill up with joy when you see the peace of an early morning sunrise, the fall leaves coloring the trees, or a pristine, glimmering waterfall? Maybe it's the vibration of a purring cat on your lap or the warmth of the family dog laying at your feet. For you, peace might be a "non-toothache" after the dentist's skills have put the pain to rest. It might be working through a conflict with your family. Peace may be the sound of a bell ringing in the cancer ward announcing that a loved one is cancer-free.

Peace is Perspective!

You are a key to guide and encourage children to expand their awareness that peace is all around them. Introducing children to people from other age groups and other cultures, who talk about their unique and personal points-of-view about peace, provides a rich tapestry for children to gain understanding of themselves and others. This builds an exciting foundation for children to stand with open hearts and embrace the many ways there are to see peace!

If we focus the attention of children in such a way that they begin to recognize peace in their lives and the lives of others, they will be inspired to continually seek peace.

I Spy Something Peaceful Game

Each person can be invited to take a turn with this game that's fun for the car, home, or classroom gatherings: One person looks around until he or she gets an idea and then says, "I spy something peaceful." The others get to guess what that person is thinking about. After they guess or are told the answer, the speaker can explain why that item is peaceful to him or her. Most of us feel happier when we "spy" peace!

Gathering Peace

Invite children to explore ways to feel, taste, hear, or touch peace. This can translate into a variety of "field trips" where everyone points out and/or gathers objects that remind them of some aspect of peace. Take care that anything gathered has already gone through most of its life cycle! Ideas are: pretty fallen leaves—pleasing my sense of beauty—acorns—reminding me of rebirth and growth—bird feathers—reminding me to be light of heart—grasses—reminding me to be flexible when in conflict, and so on. See what the children imagine!

Giving Peace

A field trip is also an opportunity to give peace to the planet by doing things as a classroom or a family such as picking up garbage or planting a tree. Frame it for the children as a way you are adding to peace or giving peace through your stewardship. Of course, we can also give peace in our relationships by demonstrating compassion or working out a conflict.

Celebrating Peaceful Conflict Resolution

Working out a conflict shouldn't make one party feel good and another bad. When all feel they have gotten back to peace and the conflict has been transformed from win-lose to win-win, then a celebration can be a key part in getting back to peace. Explore with the child (or children) ways that you can celebrate in your school or home when you succeed at working out a problem or a conflict. Then have a celebration!

Witnessing Peace

Children can be invited to speak about what they saw or did, or something they saw someone else do or say, that brought their awareness to peace. Questions and comments from the listeners create collaborative conversations at home and school and build an understanding of how peace is in our lives all the time—we just need to become aware of it.

Learning About Each Other: Sharing *Focus Moments* of Peace

Enjoy this game at bedtime. Ask the child, "How did you see peace today?" This is a wonderful way to reflect upon the day and perhaps drift off to sleep. Playing it in the car or around the family table are other good times. Share your own experiences of peace as well. Children are often surprised by some of the comments of elders. This is a way of getting to know each other more deeply. By understanding where each person sees peace, you get a glimpse of the heart and soul of that person. Often, children will want to draw about these "focus moments" in the *Peace Journal.*

Peace Journal

Invest in a scrap book and name it: *Peace Journal.* Keep it out in a family living area so anyone can record a moment of peace. Once it is full, put it on a nearby shelf like you would any other book. Children like to take these journals down just to enjoy. They often very excitedly share them with other family and friends. You are building a peace literacy legacy that will serve the family for many years to come, even for life.

Peace Place

A small table can be draped with a beautiful cloth that changes periodically to reflect a different cultural focus. Children are invited to contribute an artifact that holds a peaceful memory or represents some aspect of peace. Maybe the table holds one of the cloth napkins that was put on the dining room table when grandma and grandpa came for dinner. Perhaps it holds a book that shows characters working out a problem. Maybe it has a box of band-aids that were used to make a scrape feel better after a child's fall off a bike. It could be a place for a photo of a family event. In other words, children are inspired to be on the "look-out" for peace. They often become very enthusiastic to share. It's not uncommon for children to say, "I have something to put in the Peace Place."

Discussion Questions

- The children in the book were able to see peace in many different ways. Which picture reminded you of peace in your own life?
- Can you think of some other ways you see peace?
- Which characters did the artist show more than once in the book? What are their stories? The children often reveal their own world view as they talk about the lives of those in the pictures.
- The girl sitting under the tree has a wheelchair. What else do you think she might be finding peaceful besides the "warm sunny day"?
- The girl who is very sick in the hospital has had peace interrupted by her illness. What do you see in that picture? Do you have a sick family member who would appreciate a visit from you?
- The boy sailing objects down a gutter, after the rain has made a temporary river, finds peace as he experiences the gentle rain and enjoys his "boats." Peace is interrupted for him by someone taking his most special boat—the one he made. But he and the other child get back to peace. How do you think they did that?
- Why do you think the boy sailing the paper boat also sailed an empty soda can, rather than pick it up and recycle it? Or, do you think he did pick it up after playing with it? Why is it important to pick up our garbage? What other ideas do you have to show we care about the earth?
- The child covering her ears has had peace interrupted by a fight between her parents. On the last page she gets back to peace by going to visit her grandparents. What other ways can you think of to get back to peace in a difficult situation such as this one?
- Do you have a favorite peaceful place? Or person?
- On page 15 the girl is seeking tools to solve things peacefully. What are some of the tools she might use? (You may want to refer to the page.) This is a good time to review the conflict resolution process that your family uses or introduce the one in the poster on page 15. That poster is from *The Barnyard Buddies STOP for Peace*, also by this author.
- There are different characters in the book. If you were to make up a story about one of them, what would it be?
- How might kids in different areas around the globe seek peace?

I Smile at Myself

Julie Penshorn

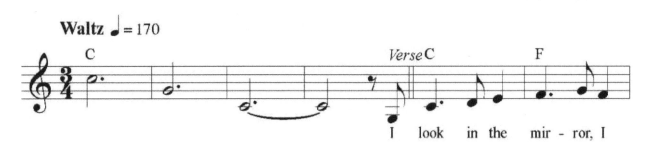

I look in the mir - ror, I

see my own face. It's the re - flec - tion of ev' - ry race. I

know peace be - gins here; it be - gins with - in.____ To ce - le - brate all life, I

give me a grin. I smile, smile, smile at my - self. Smile, smile,

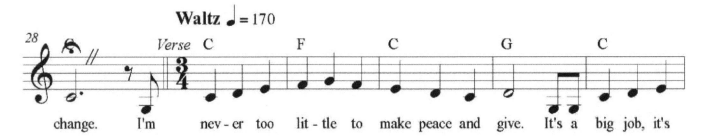

smile at my - self. Smile, smile, smile at my - self and I watch my world

change. I'm nev - er too lit - tle to make peace and give. It's a big job, it's

About the Creators

Author, Julie Penshorn, MBC is an experiential storyteller and teacher, providing key life-skills for young children in delightful children's books. Young and old alike benefit from her books which provide every-day, practical tools for coping with life's challenges and traumas.

Penshorn guides parents, grandparents, teachers, and mentors toward deeper and healthier relationships with the children in their lives, as they explore together. In this realistic portrayal, we watch resilient children celebrate the peace all around them even though they experience moments of anger, loneliness, and depression.

Penshorn, and her expert team of collaborative professionals, especially Rebecca Janke and Jeanine-Jonee Keith, realize that in order to build a culture of peace, we must work at it, one child and one story at a time.

Illustrator, Jeanine-Jonee Keith is a storyboard artist, illustrator, and instructor. She is the writer and the illustrator of the comic book, Seafoam: A Friend for Madison. A strong believer in the arts, and its importance in children's lives, Jorry runs several community-based art classes that guide children through the process of writing and drawing their own comics and books.

Content editor, Rebecca Janke, M.Ed., is a peace educator, international columnist, facilitator, community servant and leader, as well as a mentor to university students. She has over 40 years of bringing rich, unique, and practical ideas to families and educators in an entertaining and insightful manner. She specializes in integrating peace into every aspect of a curriculum.

CPSIA information can be obtained
at www.ICGtesting.com
Printed in the USA
LVHW071454080920
665351LV00027B/437